51

THALAMUS' INK.

PEGASUS BOOKS

Copyright © 2012 Thalamus' Ink.
All Rights Reserved

Copyright © 2012 by Thalamus' Ink.

All Rights Reserved. No part of this book may be produced or transmitted in any form or by any means, electronic or mechanical, including photocopying, recording or by an information storage and retrieval system—except by a reviewer who may quote brief passages in a review to be printed in a magazine or newspaper—without permission in writing from the publisher.

www.pegasusbooks.net

First Edition: March 2012

Published in North America by Pegasus Books. For information, please contact Pegasus Books c/o Ms. McGhee, P.O. Box 235, Neptune, New Jersey, 07754.

ISBN – 978-0-9832608-6-8

1. Poetry: American - African American. 2. Poetry: General

10   9   8   7   6   5   4   3   2   1

Comments about 51 and requests for additional copies, book club rates and author speaking appearances may be addressed to Thalamus' Ink. or Pegasus Books c/o Ms. McGhee, P.O. Box 235, Neptune, New Jersey, 07754, or you can send your comments and requests via e-mail to marcus.media@yahoo.com

Also available as an eBook from Internet retailers and from Pegasus Books

Printed in the United States of America

This is dedicated to the Projects where I grew up:

51 Winthrop Avenue in New Rochelle, New York.

"Dreams, Discomfort and Desire are the starting points..."

Thalamus' Ink.

MUTED OUTCRY REVISITED

Rappers singing out the cadence
Of an A-K on the pavements
And some through the flesh
It's not fresh

Parents: mother and no father
Couldn't be any harder
The only alternative is the juvey-thing
We hurt and we're hurting
Clawing for reason
But it's out of season

Little sister, just thirteen
Could have been a beauty queen
Thrust into the adult vicinity
Because she lost her virginity
Has to pay – baby's on the way

Formal ed's a veiled curtain
Headaches from hunger
Next meal uncertain
Street smarts takes care of me now
Tomorrow takes care of itself somehow

Cell to cell in my ghetto dwelling
With dust and piss for aerosols
My thoughts extend no further
Than these here walls

Born trapped and died
On this block and inside
Neither mind nor body went anywhere
Who cares?

Was that a siren outside or just the T.V.? ....
And now for a commercial

51

The sun's rays burst through worn slits in the cracked yellow window shade. I watched the sunlight pierce the bedspread and as I placed my hand there I could feel its warmth. Dust particles entered the spotlight descending and then effortlessly rising into the air like ribbons of cigarette smoke. Some of the particles remained suspended until I swept my arm through them and as if on command, the dust gave chase. I must have orchestrated their patterns for about an hour. When I pulled the shade up it snapped violently and the invading sunlight crowded every corner of the room. I squinted and could see all of the dust in chaos. Suddenly I heard my name being called and realized that this was not my first day here on earth.

For the doers:
Stevie, Mark, Joyce, Janis, Stephanie, Lynnie Boo Boo, Judy", Bubby, Cleo, Peaches, Pumpkin, Stanley, Baby Sis, Kitty Coo, Skipper, Keith, Kenard, Walter, Ann, Danny, Fetson, Robert, Diane, Beverly, Karen, Michael, Barbara, Joann, Sam and Cookie.

Thalamus' Ink.

51

Thalamus' Ink.

51

by Thalamus' Ink

Contents:

Soul Trust	1
Excursion Déjà vu	2
Penned Up	4
Black Face	5
Themes of Blackness	6
Pinching the Soul	8
In the Name Of	10
Bang Bang Bang Bang	12
Her Grace's Descent	14
Harlem Renaissance	15
Take a Number	16
Sins of our Forefathers	17
Sketches of Haiti	18
Change	20
Trickle Trickle	22
L.E.M.	24
Death Dance	25
Love Is	32
Al Jarreau	34
At Love's Touch	35
The Feast	36
Love – You Said	38
Ode to Eve	39
The Manufacturer's Warranty	40

The Players Lyric	42
With you around me	43
The Black Onus	44
Circular Breathing	47
Notes	48
Eclipse	50
Memories: Forgotten and Remembered	52
Legacy	54
Above All Love	56
A Sailors Soliloquy	57

Soul Trust

Lord
Lift my soul
Take my hand
Lead me far
From temptations land

Lord
Lift my soul
So I might see
The harm that's done
When I'm not me

Amen

Thalamus' Ink.
3/21/08

Excursion: Déjà Vu

There is certain eeriness
To this comfort
That I've found
Because I have been here before
Perhaps not yesterday
Perhaps not even
Four light years ago
And perhaps not as
My whole self
But certainly as a breeze
Or a whisper
Or a part of
Someone else's
Genetic fragment
But surely here

I recall
Many circumstances
As they have unfolded
But amnesia shrouds
The past's conclusions
Leaving vacancies
To be filled before commas
Exclamation points
Or periods
I know that I was sent

To wriggle them free
To color outside the lines
Yet introduce some order
Or direct movement towards
More navigable pursuits
For within this wake
Lies nature's kaleidoscope
Cultivating conscious life
When shaken – but it remains
Embryonic and not amphibious

Thalamus' Ink.

Penned up like lab rats
Propagating neuroses
Ghettos in lock down

Black Face

My greatest fear is being swallowed
Whole by blackness
And in the face of sadistic smiles
Or raucous and contemptible laughter
Never being heard and understood

Thalamus' Ink.
4/18/08

Themes of Blackness

A bouquet of roses
That only the
Opened box exposes

Both sun baked skin and
The smooth ebony texture reflected
As the moon's rays rush in

Work's constant sweat on my brow
The eternal bend in my back
That remains resilient somehow

My pulse racing
When at night
It's the cops I'm facing
At a streetlight

The sound of a mother's cry
When one of her children is down
And bullets still whistle by

A Saturday night drunk
Or drugs in my arm
Producing amnesia
To keep my brain from harm
Family members missing
Like a gapped toothed Jack-O-Lantern
That struggles to smile

A hole, a hole
Dug for centuries by
White folks
In order to bury my soul

Falling into an abysmal pit
And left with no heroes
To help me out of it

Pain and despair
Enduring a life time
With this bill of fare
While happiness is measured in milliseconds

Upward bound with
My ceiling's height just below the fog
That covers the ground

Thoughts of what I should
And how I could
With no one to listen

No one knows
The trouble I see
For no one feels
This "BLACK" inside me

Thalamus' Ink.
© 4/20/08

Pinching the Soul

I only stole to share I

Buried our emotions in blacks and whites

Wrapped them in tea leaves

Myself in lavenders and ruby reds

Preparing to masquerade

Proud and poised

As a beggar on Fridays

With hands now to knees

I stuck out my tush to
Stir more than air while

Working the curves and curbs

They came and paused

Flared nostrils and imprinted paws

Pressed hard and flat to glass

When the fog vanished

Juan Monet appeared

Foreign rooms all too familiar now

I threw myself naked upon the bed

Tossed my head back

Spread my legs

And tried to think of you

Thalamus' Ink.
3/28/06

In the Name of...

How can a Preacher rape a boy
In the library of the " King of Nonviolence"
Then threaten that child to buy his silence
Who do we go to pray
And here in this day
Where do we take our
Broken bodies and brains to
So that we can arrange to
Mend the remains to
Be whole again

How can we find our way to Zion
When people we should trust are lying
And only seem to have their minds on
Sins that further human imperfection
Spawned by meanness and deception
Souls splayed open without protection
Bodies like minds in need of direction
There must be a gage to control
The rage and the outrageous
Or someone to console
The afraid and be courageous
God please reign on me
So that I through you can alter their destiny
There are no winners in cruelty

Just prisoners in a system
Who will never be free
Lord, You are not dead

Thalamus' Ink
3/13/07

Bang Bang ~ Bang Bang

There's no way to say it
And not be numbed poetically
We need to delay these hits
And find a way energetically
It's time to stop
And make this huge decision
Brothers stop killing yourselves
And stop the road to prison

No brains in a bullet
It has no way to reason
Guns ~ Bros. pull it ~
As if they are in season
The very thing
They set out to prevent
Winds up too often
Killing the innocent

Oh now I hear it
The wailing of a mother
And as I feared it ~
    There's the wailing of another
Now there's a chorus
Heard loudly from outside

It's time to divorce it
Knock off this genocide

There are ribbons
For all types of cancers
Let's add another
Until we find some answers
Bang Bang with a bullet
No winner's just delusion
Bang Bang with a bullet
Brings life to a conclusion

Thalamus' Ink.
© 10/25/10

Her Grace's Descent

Maybe the sunlight that reflected her beauty
Blinded us to her perfected flaws
Or perhaps we expected far too much
Not knowing the pressure that we had caused
And that pressure shouldn't be ignored

Maybe the height of her monarchy
Fashioned vast distances from which to leap
Because our hoisted beauty queen becoming uneasy with her seat
Just dove from her pedestal – unmindful of this feat
She dissolved right into the crack on the street

Thalamus' Ink.
© 4/28/2011

Harlem Renaissance –
Psalm to Sondra K. Wilson

A Wealth of Minds, Musicians and Artists
Masses of Massive Ebony Bronzed
And I couldn't Name One on the List
For it was missed and then was gone
If my Brothers and Sisters could be hidden
That's why for four hundred years we were ridden
With slavery
Solve this mystery
Discover them and our precious History
Amen

Take A Number

In prosperity
Individuals are praised

But

In poverty
The masses are condemned

Sins of our Forefathers

Silhouette dragging
Through the back screen door
Took his place at the table's head
Prayed o'er the food
And money made
Still as a stone
Thought he was dead
Cept for the sound
Teeth gnawing on bone
Other than that
Nothing was said

Out in the morn
Chased from his bed by dawn
Fore ole sol
Sipped the dew
From the lawn
Over-alled silhouette
With lunch pail in hand
Shoulders hunched
From yesterday's load
Melting into the rutted road
Headed back to the hostile land

Thalamus'Ink.
© 6/22/11

Sketches Of Haiti

Hearts are punctured
Souls viciously torn
Turning their flesh
On the eve of dawn
Lenses focus for clarity
To frame life as it might be
As our tear stained eyes
Strain to see
The actual footage
Of the earthquake in Haiti
The blood dyed life of others
Compacted concrete crushed
Sisters and brothers
Mothers bleed out in tears
Listen to their wailing cries
Praying to the Father
Asking him why
Praying to God
To calm their fears
Then trusting that their prayers
Sung out as hymns
Will deliver their loved ones
Back to them
Hope - is a groan
Heard under masonry
Yesterday it was buildings and schools
Squalid conditions now breed chaos

And if chaos now rules – We hear
Feed me and my family first
And the water –
Who has the greater thirst?
A child, the wounded -
A nation allegedly cursed
Parched by neglect and poverty
The fore and aft of Haiti

Lenses see but shield our noses
That putrid smell is no bed of roses
Human carrion is the catch of the day
1,000s upon 1,000s are the fields of decay
Winds capture then vomit the smell
All that inhale it taste the tale that it tells
That gutters can't offer coffins for all
No markers no crosses not even a stone
Like dying on foreign soil so far from home
And now – through the rubble
The corpuses are counted
In the future the blessings will be too
But on a day when so many deaths mounted
And the dust drowned out a sky of blue
Wedged between death and desperation
Were a people who loved life like you and me
Who endure this portrait of daily devastation
That won't go away by turning off a TV

Thalamus' Ink.
© !/ 19 / 10

Thalamus' Ink.

The weight of history has seized my mind
Holding fast too many yesterdays
When Blacks were brought captured and bound
In the hulls of ships and then hauled away

The weight of history has seized my mind
In times when Blacks were thought of as apes
Only worthy a plantation to work
Never as an equal with a future to shape

The weight of history has seized my mind
The beatings the hangings and the rapes
Half bred children enslaved for housework
The Black ones fielded until the sun's wake

The weight of history has seized my mind
About Black bloodshed for this land's wars
Of how proudly we fought and continued to serve
Protecting laws you thought we didn't deserve

The weight of history has seized my mind
The struggle for freedom – just for a seat
And for the right to an education
An untapped source that might fuel a nation

The weight of history has seized my mind
For freedom presents possibilities
Of doctors and lawyers and even CEO's
In Black numbers unimaginable to me

The weight of history has seized my mind
Upon these shoulders sit my ancestors
They forged a path when none existed
On this day I wish they here could witness

The weight of history has seized my mind
For Obama on One-Twenty of 09
Our First Black President of our U.S.A.
And now where am I these scars to lay
And where am I now those scars to lay
Perhaps   at last   to bed...

Change

Trickle Trickle Trickle - My Ass

While the Pres is trying - people are still dying
Senators are still lying and I sit up here frying
While we try to cope they
Got us cramped up under their microscope
Watching to see how we stretch a dollar
While they raise the interest, credit cards and tuition
They're trying to kill off all of our ambition
To be somebody

Yes we got an ebony Pres but
They put him into a black hole
And hope that there he'll rest
While banks watch the economy fold
Money ain't trickled down to me
Ain't trickled down a damn cent to me
And asking me to pay for this liberty
From a jail with the invisible bars
With no windows at night
To peer out and see the stars

There's nothing to give me hope
They're worried bout passing health care
When I can't even get off welfare
There's nothing to help me cope
As I keep looking for a job that pays
But it must be on Mars
The only numbers that I see clearly

Are the numbers that ring in my ears dearly
Three children and a wife to feed
Rent and automobile unpaid
Everyone is gravely in need
While the Repo man proudly struts out of the shade

Every ten seconds the phone rings
And the voice at the other end sings:
"Dear sir, we have found
That it's our time to stand our ground
Upon which you are sinking
Yes we are going to stand on poverty's head
Because that's America's way of thinking"
And for me - I'm bled
Trickle down money what a wonderful sound
It's a lie because it carries no truth
Trickle down money can't be passed down
Because there's not even a leak in the roof
And the proof remains
Like Adam in the beginning:
I'm bare and with less than a fig leaf
To cover things

Thalamus' Ink.
12/14/09

L.E.M.

Lately
There are no closets
To shut warped desires in
These ravenous thoughts grope
For surfaces to cling to
Then consciously claw
For the faintest crevice of hope
Those womb beggars' elbow and knee

Inside
This bone cold cocoon
This stark still arthritic construct
By ideations fueled
I endure each orbit's decay and
Struggle to survive frigid Februarys
While anticipating Spring's acceptance
Still I feel so far from home

Thalamus' Ink.
© 8/9/10

Death Dance

Fear blanketed Ali's room like a coastal fog. It was suffocating him. At first his nervous energy had been put to good use as he made up his bed, did his homework. He had even swept the floor. Now with nothing else to do he sat frozen in the chair in his room and waited. What had seemed an eternity ended as a deep voice at the door interrupted the dead silence in the apartment. His father's voice, even in a whisper, echoed down the hallway like distant thunder. This impending storm was too close to calm an eight year old - He sat there drew a deep breath and started to tremble.

Who had ever had a perfect day? A day like that, a day where everything went right, it did not exist in Ali's world. A few minutes then passed and his mother summoned him to the dinner table. After a brief blessing over the pork and beans his father started asking questions for which he already knew the answers. He must have talked to mom just before they were seated. Ali hated these dinners because it always served as an introduction to a card game in which he had the losing hand. The stakes were always too high. Showdown was about to begin:

"*Ali, What did you do today?*" his father asked.
A sheepish "*Nothing really Dad*" was uttered just above a whisper and answers like that always demanded a further explanation.
"*Nothing? Did you clean your room?*"
"*No*". (Fear had made him forget). "*No, What?*"
"*No, Sir Dad*".
"*Boy, You better learn how to talk to me*".
"*Yes Sir Dad*".
What happened to your mother's money from the grocery store?"
"*Oh, Henry, it was just about twenty-cents*".
His mother was trying desperately to defuse a fire that was clearly out of her hands.
"*I lost some of it.*"
And yesterday's home work?"
"*I handed it in?*"
"*But what grade did you get?*"
"*An F*.
"*And did you come directly home from school today like I told you??!!*"
"*Well, I forgot dad.*"
"*You forgot??!!*"

Ali's fathers continued to raise his voice almost in octaves as he spoke but in a very controlled manner. It was as if he were practicing musical scales, like some baritone, only through clenched teeth. His jaws flaunted muscles that could have been the biceps on any average person.

"*Go straight to your room and wait for me. I'll be right back there!*"

Ali reached his room at a sprinter's pace.

The time that had elapsed from his father's last words "right back there" until ... seemed like another eternity or perhaps this was just another long pause from the last one. His fear returned and intensified. His throat was desert dry and Ali tried to swallow but a mass the size of his fist prevented him. He could feel his throat swelling and constricting at the same time. His own spit seemed to scratch and cut as he tried again to swallow. His breathing quickened and became twice as difficult and his heart was pounding so loud and hard that he thought it would burst right through his chest. Clothes were sticking to him as if he'd been swimming in them. Ali wiped the sweat from his forehead. The window shade was pulled down in his room and the poorly lit hallway only framed the open doorway leaving Ali to drown in its airless darkness. Ali's father had always demanded that he stand at attention in the middle of the room like a soldier until he arrived. His legs had tired from standing so long and he resorted to leaning against the bed. He could feel his fear multiplying and wiped the sweat from his forehead. Ali's memory had not been addled however and he punished himself over and over again; recalling only two nights ago what again would soon ensue.

After what appeared to be an hour, Ali figured that surely his dad was trying to psyche him out or had forgotten all together. He wanted to believe the latter. He changed into his pajamas and then kneeled at the bedside and began to pray. He prayed for a long time too. "Amen. And thank you God for making dad forget." Ali felt relieved as he eased himself to his feet. He turned toward the poorly lit hallway the light stared over a huge hulking shadow exposing a wide black leather belt held high to the ceiling. Quicker than light speed his father had grabbed Ali's arm with his left hand and held it in a vice grip as *SHAP, SHAP, SHAP, SHAP* rang out like gunshots. The sound ricocheted from wall to wall and just above the echoes an enraged thunderous voice yelled out over and over again:

"*You're going to obey me! You're going to obey me, or I'll kill you!*"

A flood of tears trailed the realization of what was occurring only after Ali's first involuntary screams and leaps, through the white-hot shock of pain.

"Yes Sir Daddy, Yes Sir Daddy, I Will" Ali cried out as he began to run in circles. It felt as if blood were running down his legs with each of his father's savage strokes. Ali burst into a full gallop, circling like a rogue horse on a carousel. Around and up, gallop, leap and gallop; around and down gallop, dive; gallop were the movements it initiated. Ali tried to catch his breath. Spurred on by the encouragement of his dad's powerful and tireless right arm this endless waltz continued in 6/8 time. Each volley of *SHAP, SHAP, SHAP, and SHAP* sent out jolts of electricity that cut through his clothes splaying his skin down to the white of the bone from his head to the toes. *"Yes Sir Daddy, Yes Sir Daddy, I promise, Please Daddy!"* Ali pleaded as he tried to cover himself.

"Daddy, Daddy, I promise to do better! I promise Daddy!" were automatic responses to the pain but his father, who must have summoned his strength from some unholy source, had grown deaf in the process.

"Daddy, I'll do better, please" were Ali's last words, his shrill cries in time weakened to a whisper and then he was silent. His father continued to exact his anger on the child from head to his toe and then back again until Ali finally fell to the floor. There would be no more tears – they had been completely exhausted.

Ali's mouth was wide open and although the dried blood about his cracked lips wasn't chocking him, air refused to rush in or out. Whether he had mustered his last ounce of strength to get to his feet again or his father had hoisted him up, Ali was now too weak to stand or even move and fell back to the floor vulnerable; still his father showered him with a hundred thousand more volts of pain.

That wide black belt continuously found its destination. It's shrill *SHAP, SHAP, SHAP, SHAP* sound echoed from body to wall, penetrating through into the next room bringing no response from the recipient. Ali's mother wept aloud but her cries could not be heard. She felt every vicious lash herself and recoiled in anticipation of the next. It had never helped for her to try and intervene; in fact, it only seemed to make things worse. She prayed that this would quickly run its course but had no idea how far it was from the start or end of its eternity. The carousel now teetered at a slower pace with its rogue horse now beaten and broken – and still the beating continued. Ali's body refused to hurt any more. His nerves were without impulses but his father continued on with his belt hand still dedicated to its task. There was no more pain because pain had become yesterday's servant. Ali, now distant from himself, sat and watched from his perch in the far corner of his room. He was almost apathetic about this massacre as the predator finally crushed the windpipe of his prey. With his victim now lifeless Henry Hanson drew back his weapon through its belt looped scabbard and retired from his son's room. Like nightfall, the shadow gradually receded down the hallway as its voice heaved, *"You're going to obey me! You're going to obey me."* This thunder reverberated off into the distance while in disaster's wake, Ali watched himself lay lifeless on the floor. He wondered if he was truly dead and if not would he return back to this tattered form or be freer without it? Then, suddenly, he felt himself sigh and heard his own whimpering again.

Thalamus' Ink.
© 9/14/10

Love Is...

Love is sunrises as well as rainy days
Love is light shining right through the dense fog's haze

Love is the smile on an innocent child's face
Love is love's vulnerability without feeling any disgrace

Love is fresh kisses given each and every day
Love is roses for those kisses when I am away

Love is what happens after love has been made
Love is playing together and never being played

Love is the first tears when your newborn cries
Love is those same tears when grown they say goodbye

Love is an open hand instead of a clenched fist
Love is knowing in this heart that you will always exist

Love is belief when few would ever dare
Love is the answer to a desperate person's prayer

Love is an image placed upon your soul
Love is the essence of what really makes us whole

Love is never me but Love is always us
Love is giving all of yourself and learning how to trust

Thalamus' Ink.

Al Jarreau come blow
Sing a song that fills my sails
Riff me back to Spain

At Love's Touch

Receptive hearts use less eyes
Sur render trust to braille
Feel the lune
Trace the stars oer heavens omni verse
Notes yet played but now X pressed
Tack tile ardor smooth and cool
Then cool and splen door warm
Opened to trust U
Brush U
Then slow the knead
To be intent shun all
And tran sit shun
Into well combed
Glis sin ings
As we lay
Sigh ted pre X stacy

Thalamus' Ink.
© 10/25/11

THE FEAST

Warm in the middle
With a zephyr
Swirling about
Delighting my periphery

Grounded - yet as light
As in flight as I can be
With Oscar tickling the ivories
Sunday afternoon in the N.Y.C.

Dinner's bouquets wafting with his notes
Drifting through the windows
As easily as black keys he denotes
Helium filled - headed for the Hamptons

Fills the humid air
Easily as it fills my ears
Begs to be caressed and shared
Beckons to be free and heard
Not blared
That would be absurd

Hard to decipher the complexity
Of which hunger

Will first be
Sated as I've sat and waited
Immovable
Til the interlude

Thalamus' Ink.

Love - You said love

Love is sometimes
Just starting out real slow
As slow as the Spring's sunshine
Melts the Winter's snow
Love is sometimes
The love that makes you blush
Then realizing it doesn't require touch
Love is sometimes
From sunup to sundown
Love is sometimes
That smile that hides a frown
Love is sometimes
Not saying how you feel
Love is sometime
Feeling that this love isn't real
Love is sometimes
From birth til far past gray
Love is sometimes
Being wise enough
To be silent and staying away...
T'J.

Ode to Eve

Walls ceilings
Corners and bars
Are the spoils of your love
And its rewards
These urban artifacts
These Manmade constructs
Only blunt and burden
A heart whose soul
Had always deduced
That its only purpose
Was to love you

Alone - I find myself
Riddled with gravity
Unable to inspire
Tired and weak
Subsisting within endless forms of
Walls ceilings corners and bars
Flightless now with snare secured
You seized an energetic virgin spirit
Prostituting it and myself as well
To replicate Adam's descent
When first he envisioned himself - human

Thalamus' Ink.
© 2/13/07

The Manufacturer's Warranty

Corridors were where we met
In narrow spaces of time
That filled times crevices
And sated our appetites
That quenched our thirsts
And filled in life's imperfections
That makes us all imperfect
And yet made it perfect for the moment
Because there is no air in a vacuum

The truths that we allowed ourselves
Were always kept secret and to ourselves
Lest separate worlds collide
And though ours was the smaller world
We invested more time
In our perfect painless oasis
Designed for brain and body escapes
Scripted by the panacea's medicinal cure
And rewarded by our personal applause
For perfect acts played out in corridors

Perfection has conditions
Sets its rules – makes its own demands
Still there's no air in a vacuum
And so we held our breath each time
Until transitioned into humans flawed

Then inhaling the air filled stench of smog
Perhaps the odors that were caused
By the residues left out in corridors
The only source of air to breath
Which flawed this perfection that we conceived

Thalamus' Ink.
© 12/7/09

The Player's Lyric

I have loved so many women
And
                They have loved me as well
                I have loved too many women
                And spent some time in hell
                Well,
                At least for a spell

With you around me
I'm as tall as skyscrapers
Poking holes in clouds

The Black Onus: For Hope in the Future

It is our responsibility
To grow ears as receptive
As the arid earth is to rainwater
To absorb knowledge from oceans
And listen to the sounds of education
Until we no longer thirst

It is our responsibility
To direct both eyes and minds
To focus on a future
That has a future
Which builds confidence, integrity,
Trust and happiness

It is our responsibility
To adhere to one another
And to pull each other
Toward the positive
And witness life's ultimate high
Born of self esteem, accomplishment
And community

It is our responsibility
To know, to preach about and to avoid
Anything whose inherent powers

Have failed to recreate family
Family is the educator in the art of
Love, respect and teachings
Elders are the seers
Who through experience
And selflessness
Help us to erect bridges
Over the deepest
And darkest canyons in our lives

It is our responsibility
To revive the sense of community
For we have
Through arrogance, ignorance or neglect
Lost at least a generation
And lost generations largely birth lost souls
Many unloved many neglected
Many are just numbed
Community therefore, by adaptation, rededication
Or by adoption - must return

It is our responsibility
To stand erect and not to cower
To assume the posture
That brings us favorably into the light
And to shout until we are heard
To renew hope and the sense of community

Thalamus' Ink.

Where opportunity is to everyone's advantage
And where the pursuit of happiness
Requires no walls, no locks, no fists and no arms
Requires no walls, no locks, no fists and no arms
Either physically or otherwise
It is our responsibility

Thalamus' Ink.
© 5/20/09

Circular Breathing

Parched brown lifeless leaves
Colored kites blown by Autumn's breeze
Prisoner's freed from half nude trees
Inevitable victims of the season's disease

On the lam life swept away
Leaves subjected to decay
Arboreal skeletons shivered and prayed
That at their root - life was saved

Winters chill held Natures breath
Creating a bed so she could rest
She tossed and turned as you can guess
For all She craved was a warm caress

Abruptly from slumber enrapt with Spring
She breathed Summer into everything
By Autumn she'd wonder how much she'd done
For parched brown leaves again had come

Thalamus' Ink
2/27/06

Notes

Oh Resilient Sisters and Brothers
I am happy to find you whole
And not just the sum of your parts
For the philistines are incapable of happiness
Setting a higher price on their body counts
Leaving no field fallow
And no one out of season

The house and the field are distant but prevalent visions
That the richness of the green predominates and
Begets the limpest of handshakes, the faintest commitments
The greatest insincerity and erects the tallest walls
Intent on the one eighty
Resurrecting both manor and moat
Restoring menial labor
Reviving hymns in fields of futility

It is important for all of us
That you succeed
That you breathe the fresh air and
Allow your focus to extend
Much farther than its periphery
And utilize your imagination
To command those imaginings to materialize

Blood of mine we have birthed so many children
And reared so few

We have germinated in the darkness
And niggardly clung to the shade
Let us thrust our children out into the light
Nurtured with love, education and the motivation
To cure generations of ills
To eliminate the stunting
Of Ideas, ideals and the life we deserve

Should you waver or perhaps stumble
My voice or hands serve only
To reassure this commitment and
To place you squarely back on your path
So that you can touch so many others
That my hands or voice couldn't reach
Let us ignite ideas to frame sound tomorrows
While permitting our fields the time to lay fallow
Returning life back to nature's course
So that life may be lived again

Thalamus' Ink.
© 12/01/08

Eclipse
(The Galactic Hiccup)

Night Light
Venture out onto
Heaven's scape
Shimmering astral rays
Glitter in attendance
Ignoring the vastness of the void
While parting cumulus haze
Hushed winds to a whisper
Hid novas
Held pursed lips
All from shadows

Pearl - Ole Sol
In full moon's mirror
White Luminous glow
No less inferior
Bled to burnt orange
Like the eve
Extending into night
A confounding yet soothing sight
Confirming a Magicians
Hand of slight

In reflection or deflection or obscurity
In the vastness and the crassness

Of this galaxy
Such moments can serve to reflect
That life and its close calls
Demand respect
That beauty in life
Its brightness may be
Reflected, hidden or bent
But eventually reveals itself
Again most radiant

Thalamus' Ink.
© 12/21/10

Memories: Forgotten and Remembered

Fragrance from dried petals of yesterdays since fled
Discovered in leaves inadvertently disturbed while nestled
in their bed
And for some reason now obscure
Were entrusted to insure
That love in its virginity
Had never left this vicinity
Neither in psyche or physically
And now reopened I can see
The memories rushing back to me

Oh to be
The on rush of spring
As winter had to flee
Denuding its victims – thawed to the skin
Vulnerable to Spring's more gentle wind
While summer offered more susceptible sins
And a limber mind to cope with them
And a body as limber as well
Whose ventures could then skirt
The edges of hell

Callous celebrations in fall life
If prolonged
Brings forth more strife
Rupturing clouds bringing sleet and rain
Bellowing thunder to proclaim life's pains

Tears remember the season's change
So that we can cope with them
And us again
Now having taken this second look
Carefully the petals were returned to their book

Legacy

A Smile
That warm and tender smile
Injected sunshine into our faces
Lighting up the darkest places

A Voice
That always held my ear
Filled with knowledge
And good cheer

A hand
So gentle yet so very firm
That held my reins
Until I learned

A Manner
Such a suave mien
Honey coated
Though very keen

A Love
That grew from the very first day
Which swelled through life's storms
And couldn't be washed away

A promise
Asked and devotion kept

And never did you lose your step
A father's trust in the father's son
Though now one rest
The others not done

Life is but a promise kept
The terms of the promise
Seem out of step
With what we feel should be our time
That's why God draws the blinds
And then it is at last to sleep
The lucky ones are able to peek
Again- A Smile

Thalamus' Ink.

Thalamus' Ink.

Above all love
Without it, what breath merits the next
And the soul be but an open empty chiasm
Protected from hearts investments
A museum, which screens all but two senses
The innocent virgin unaware that there are fences

Above all love
That permits the minds levity
And the heart to canter and gallop
At unreasonable paces
On worn roads and through untrod fields
With equal certainty

Above all love
That insists that reason not govern
Yet act as the emissary to emotions
Which beg to be commanded
Knowing that this heart will cushion its fall
If this love requires any gravity at all

Above all love

A Sailors Soliloquy

Why have You not gone
Though touch by distance be chilled
And the last warm zephyr exhaled
Fetid skin and hull portend
Of a mind and soul's erosion
All but abandoned now
I concede to this condemned vessel

In its final performance
Rudderless and unfit for mast
Its voyage over many seas remained
Steadfast and logged into this eulogy
Through turbulent Atlantic's
And placid Pacific's
Still You inhabit my keel

Thalamus' Ink.
11 / 15 / 06

www.ingramcontent.com/pod-product-compliance
Lightning Source LLC
Chambersburg PA
CBHW031423040426
42444CB00005B/688